# Copyright & Disclaimer

# About Maxwell Fox

With a taste for adventure, Maxwell Fox has always been passionate about one thing: traveling.

Ever since he was a little boy he was filled with a unique curiosity and an adventurous spirit that took him along to beautiful and amazing new experiences. From short trips with family to imaginary travels around the world, his wanderlust was his driving force from a young age.

He was fascinated by the endless possibilities of new lands, people and ways of life and that is exactly what he looked to discover every time he went on a new adventure.

From trying the local cuisine and exploring brand new flavors, to visiting all the important cultural and historical sights, he carefully planned each trip so he could experience each place to the fullest and discover every little corner.

What he was after was not the tourist experience but the unique immersion into a new community and a different culture.

So what he did was strive to experience each city like a true local.

Traveling gave him the opportunity to increase his knowledge and interest in history, culture, art, architecture and language. Through his experiences he sought to improve his skills and become the best version of himself.

After his many adventures and life changing experiences, he tried to find a path that would excite him just as much as traveling did.

So he thought of what travelers everywhere have in common and what thing brings all his interests together. And that's how he started his journey through the artful science of cartography.

With a formal training in cartography and a unique love for traveling and adventure, Maxwell Fox decided to make it his life's mission to help fellow travelers around the world have the most amazing experience every time they travel.

## ACCOMMODATION

 Hotel

 Motel

 Hostel

 Camping

## FOOD & DRINK

 Restaurant

 Fast food

 Cafe

 Ice cream

 Bar

 Pub

## SHOP & SERVICE

 Supermarket

 Deperment store

 Marketplace

 Kiosk

 Greengrocer

 Alcohol

 Confectionery

 Bakery

 Tea

 Electronics

 Computer

 Mobile

 Hifi

 Clothes

 Shoes

 Jewellery

 Bag

 Beauty

 Perfumery

 Hairdresser

 Laundry

 Travel agency

 Books

 Art

 Gift

 Toys

 Florist

## TRANSPORTATION

 Parking

 Taxi

 Bus stop

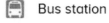 Bus station

 Subway entrance

 Rental car

 Fuel

 Charging station

 Rental bicycle

 Aerodrome

 Helipad

 Ferry

## ENTERTAINMENT, ARTS & CULTURE

 Cinema

Theatre

| | | | |
|---|---|---|---|
| ♫ | Nightclub | | **LAND USE** |
| 🏛 | Museum | ▬▬▬ | Highway |
| 📖 | Library | ▬▬▬ | Primary road |
| 👤 | Artwork | ▬▬▬ | Secondary road |
| 🎨 | Arts Center | ▬▬▬ | Tertiary road |
| ⛲ | Fountain | ▬▬▬ | Unclassifield road |
| ✳ | Viewpoint | ▬▬▬ | Railway |
| | | ▬▬▬ | Tram railway |
| | **FINANCIAL** | - - - - | Ferry road |
| 🏧 | Atm | ▬▬▬ | Water |
| 💵 | Bank | ▬▬▬ | Beach |
| | | ▲ | Volcano |
| | **ACTIVITY** | ▬▬▬ | Border |
| 🏃 | Fitness | ▬▬▬ | Quarry |
| 🏊 | Swimming | ▬▬▬ | Comemercial |
| 🏌 | Golf | ▬▬▬ | Nature |
| | Miniature golf | ▬▬▬ | Park |
| | Playground | ▬▬▬ | Residential area |
| | **HEALTHCARE** | | **OTHER** |
| ⊕ | Hospital | 🛈 | Information |
| | Doctor | 🚻 | Toilets |
| | Pharmacy | | Waste basket |
| 🦷 | Dentist | | Drinking water |
| 👓 | Optician | | Table |
| | | | Bench |
| | **POST** | | Elevator |
| ✉ | Post box | | Police |
| | Post office | 🔥 | Fire station |
| | | ⚖ | Courthouse |
| | | 🚩 | Embassy |

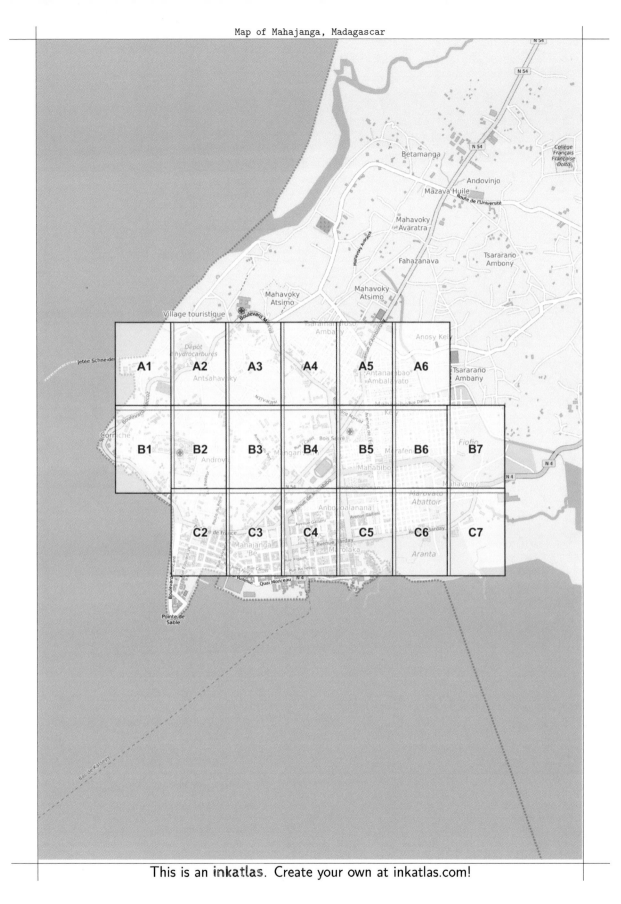

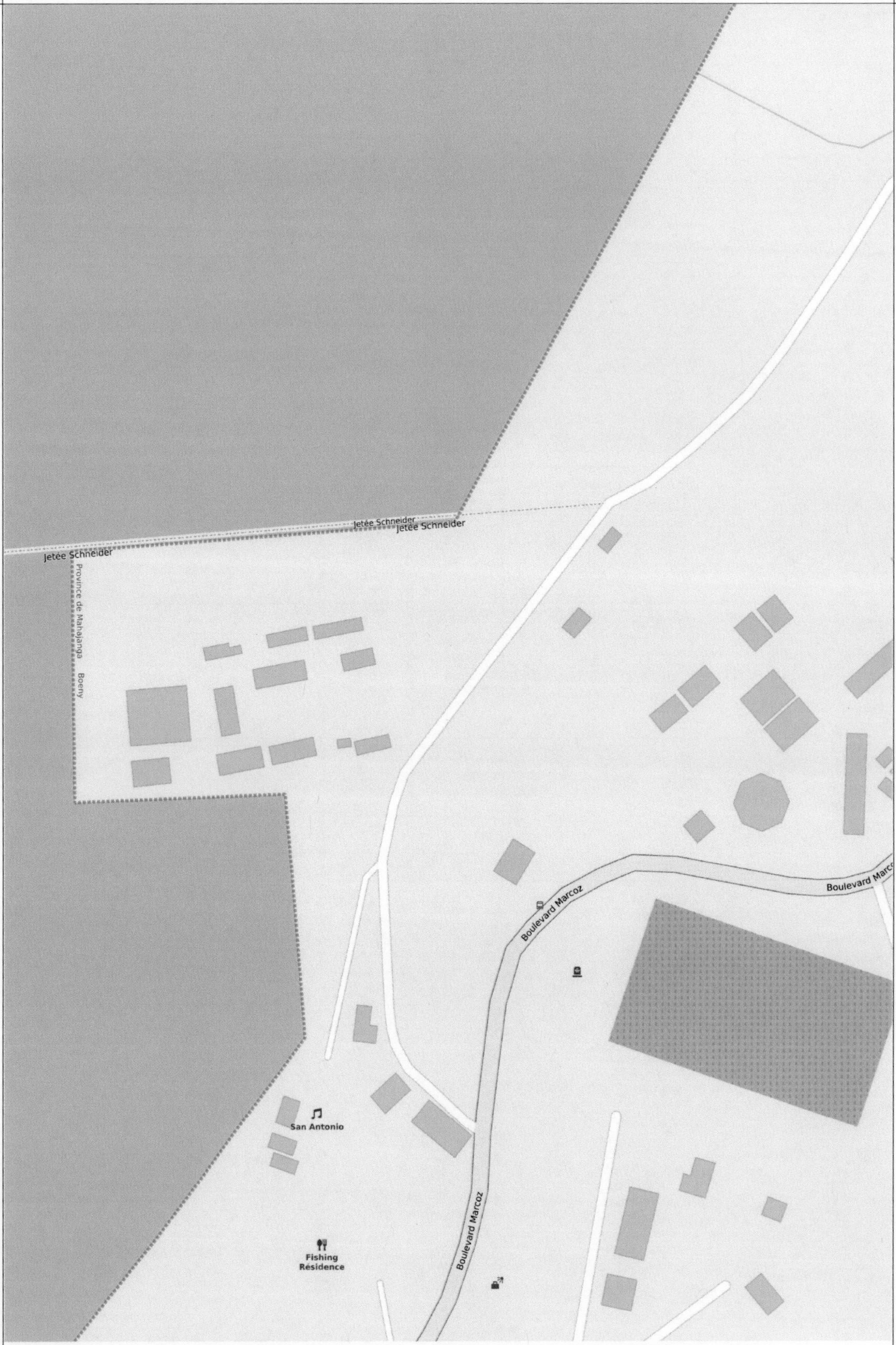

Jetée Schneider
Jetée Schneider
Jetée Schneider

Province de Maholanga

Boeny

A2

Boulevard Marcoz

Boulevard Marcoz

Boulevard Marcoz

San Antonio

Fishing
Résidence

▽ B1 ▽

Plage

Camelia
Village

Route Village Touristique

Anjara
Hotel

Boulevard Marcoz

Dépôt
d'hydrocarbures

Boulevard Marcoz

Solima

Boulevard Marcoz

Lycée
technique
et professionnel
Mahajanga

Boulevard Marcoz

Chez Narindra

Created on Inkatlas. © OpenStreetMap contributors (openstreetmap.org). Map data Dec 02, 2018. 1:2500

◁
A2
◁

▷
A4
▷

Tribunal
d'appel

EPP Fiharovana

Complexe
sportif
de Mahajanga

Boulevard Marcoz

Croisement
Bloc

M3TV-M3FM

M3TV-M3FM

Boulevard Marcoz

Cyber
Multi-Services

École
Catholique
Coeur
Immaculé
de Marie

Clinique
Médico
Chirurgicale

Boulevard Marcoz

Lycée
Privé
FJKM
Ziona
Vaovao

FJKM Ziona
Vaovao

Boulevard Marcoz

Na-Cha

Boulevard Marcoz

Collège
Montfort
Saint-
Gabriel

Avenue Phi

La Tavern

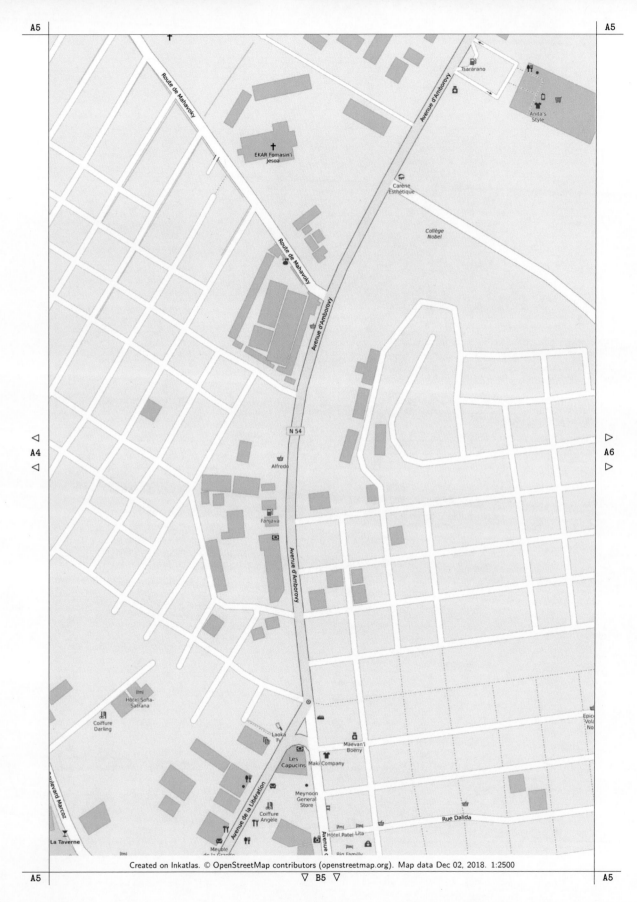

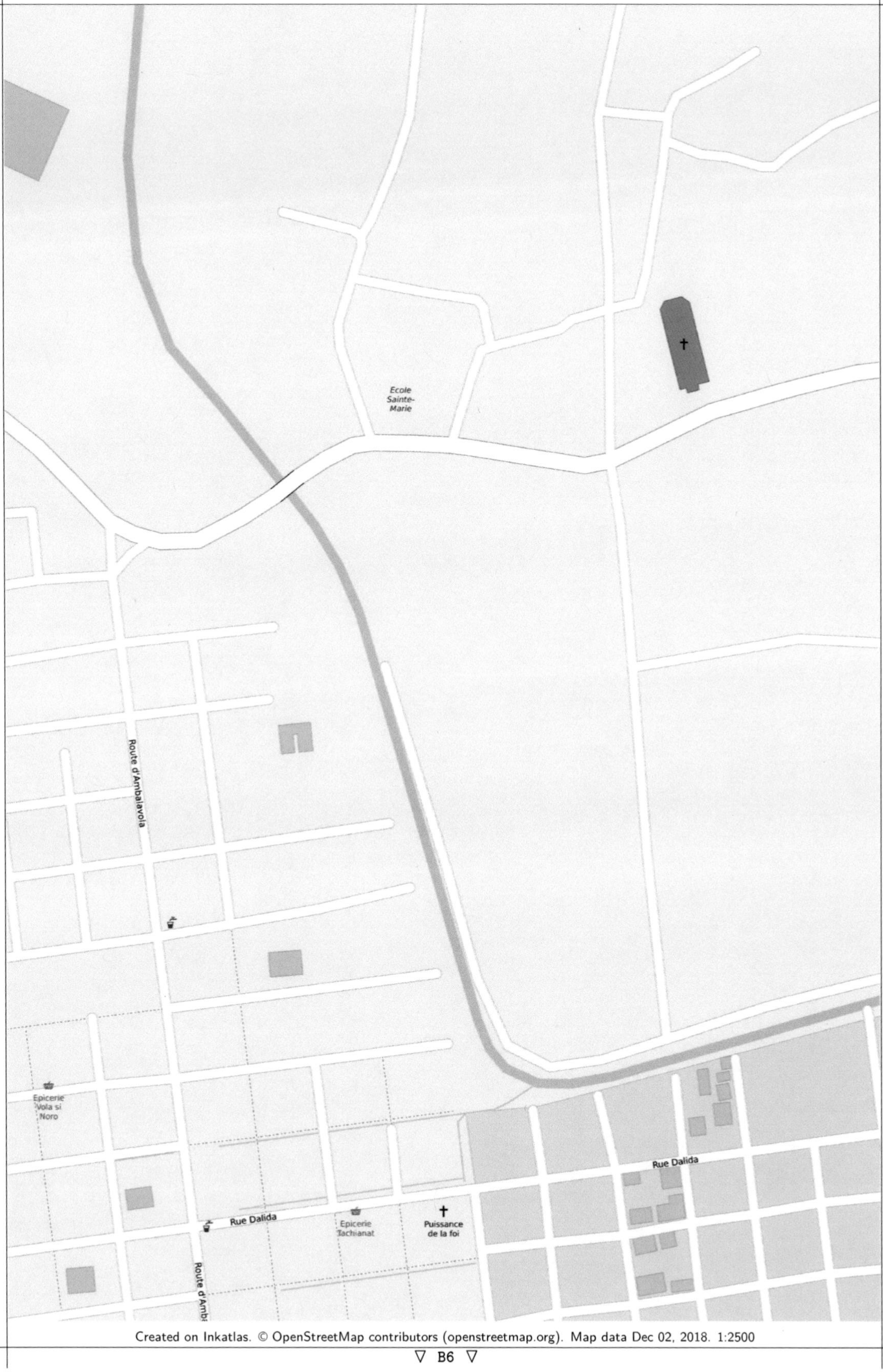

Ecole
Sainte-
Marie

†

Route d'Ambalavola

Epicerie
Vola si
Noro

Rue Dalida

Route d'Amb

Epicerie
Tachianat

†
Puissance
de la foi

Rue Dalida

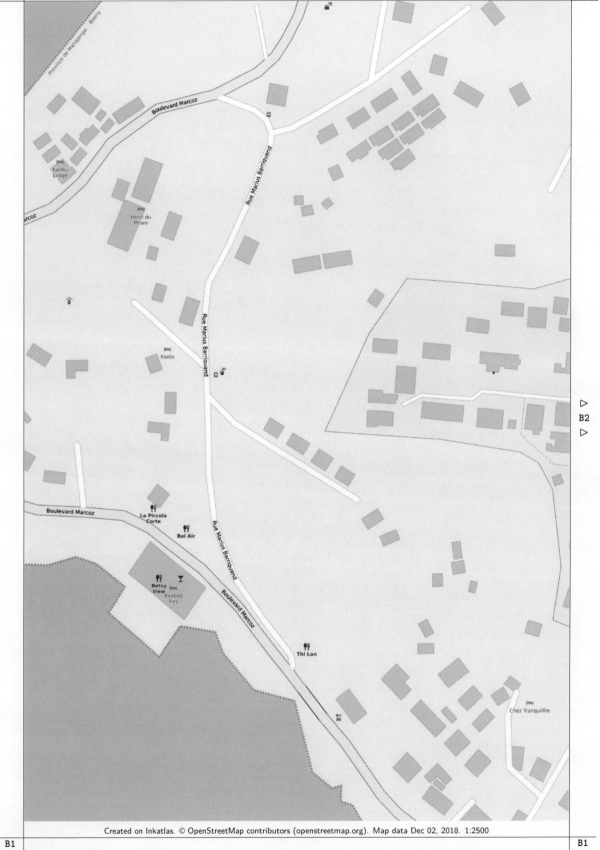

Service
Pédiatrie

service
radiologie

Complexe
Mère Enfant

Urgences

Institut
de formation
inter
régional
des paramédicaux
Mahajanga

Complexe
Mère Enfant

Complexe
Mère Enfant

Aumônerie
Androva

Pose de
la première
pierre
du Centre
Régional
de Transfusion
Sanguine

Pharmacie
hospitalière

Chez Gaëlle

Rue Pasteur

FJKM Androva
Vaovao

Villa Mena

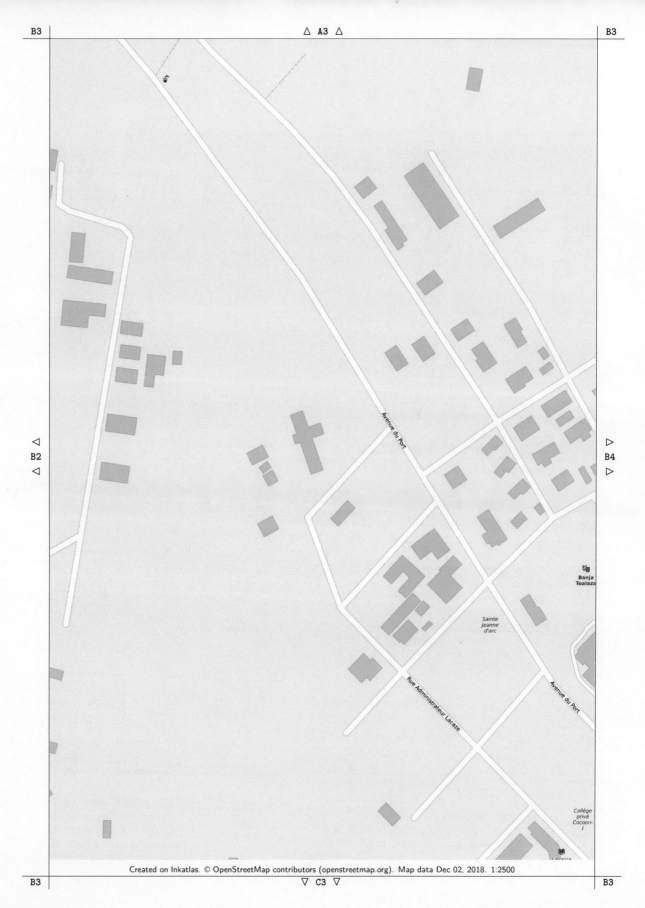

Avenue du Port

Banja
Toalaza

Sainte
Jeanne
d'arc

Rue Administrateur Lacaze

Avenue du Port

Collège
privé
Cocoon-
I

Librairie

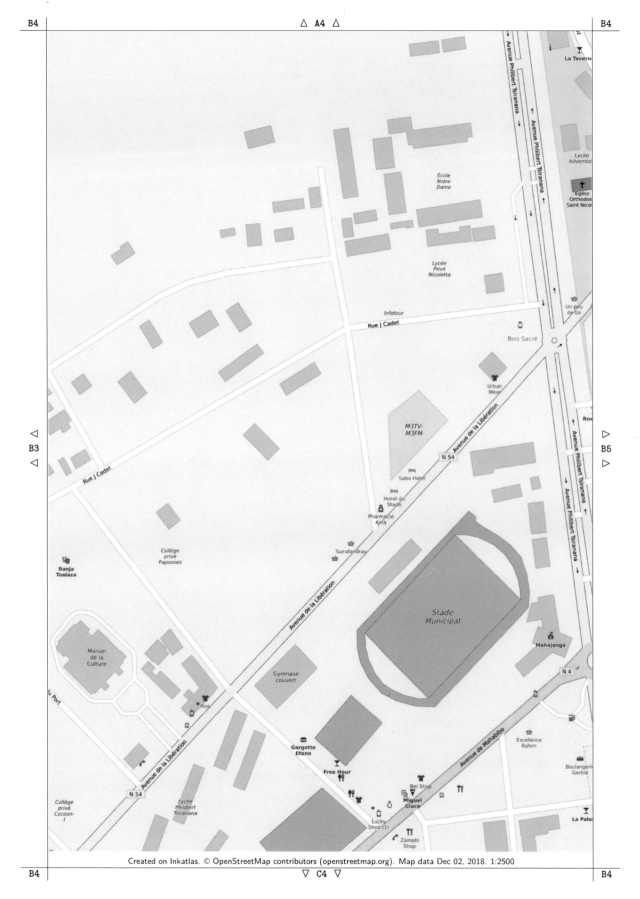

Rue Dalida

Hôtel Patel Lita
Big Family

La Taverne

Comore
Angèle

Meuble
de la Grande
Ile

Chic Beauté
2

Syldi

Tohanaina
Salala

Salala
Hotel

N 54
Boulevard Marcoz

Pharmacie
Belvédère

Lycée
Adventiste

Buvette
Mamabe

Blé d'Or

Épicerie
Bayah

Eglise
Orthodoxe
Saint Nicolas

Hôpital
Mahabibo

Najmi
Generale
Store

Un peu
de toi

Manga

Pharmacie
Anjarasoa

Jiva

Boulangerie
Moderne

Roxette

Buvette
Lafatra

Mr. Bean

Coiffure
Lydia

Monaco

JHM Hôtel

Chez Matardi

Mora Prix

EKAR Mahabibo

DMT Photo

Sava

Fulaic

Chez Mme
Chabaud

Bijouterie
Coco

Commissariat
de Police

Police
Municipale

Hotel

Store

Mada
Hôtel

Salala
(3)

EGC Hatim

Kissor

La ménagère

Snack
Pizzéria
Le Roi

I 4

Number
One

Mosquée
Chadhouli

Hôtel Soalala

Mahela

Boulangerie
Gerblé

Dallas

Mosquée
du Vendredi

Safar'inn
Hôtel

Ambovoalanana

La Paloma

Le Majunga

Chez Ali
Baba

Avenue de l'Église
Avenue de la Libération
Avenue Philibert Tsiranana
Avenue Philibert Tsiranana
Avenue de l'Église
Avenue des Comores
Avenue du 14 oc
Avenue du 14

Route d'Ambalavola

Epi-Bar
Mamokatra

Poteau-
Be

Épicerie
Gasikara

Mosquée
Ambalavola

Route d'Ambalavola

Hôtel Eclipse

Coiffure
7/7

Bar Dombolo

Coiffeur
Original
Jeck Man

Trois
étoiles

29 mars
1947

EPP Mahabibo
Fiofio

Mey

ala
)

Created on Inkatlas. © OpenStreetMap contributors (openstreetmap.org). Map data Dec 02, 2018. 1:2500

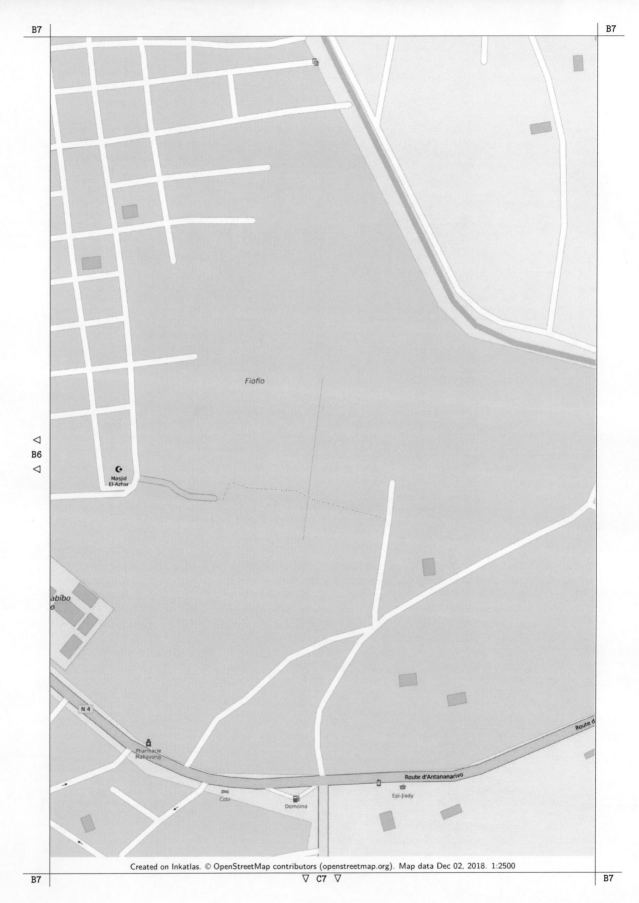

Fiofio

Masjid
El-Azhar

abibo
o

N 4

Pharmacie
Mahavony

Route d

Route d'Antananarivo

Cobi

Domoina

Epi-Jiady

Created on Inkatlas. © OpenStreetMap contributors (openstreetmap.org). Map data Dec 02, 2018. 1:2500

Rue Pasteur

Route du Rova

Rue Pasteur

Province de Mahajanga Boeny

Boeny Province de Mahajanga Boeny

Boulevard Poincaré

Boulevard Poincaré

Boulevard Poincaré

Boulevard Poincaré

Bouye be

Avenue de France

Rue du Jardin Public

BFV

Avenue de France

Lemizo Bar Restaurant Malagasy

InformaTIC bureau

CEG Charles Renel

Buro-Service

Fun Bouti

La Ruche

Université de Mahajanga

Art Coiffure

Rue de Belgique

Rue Hubert

La Toile

Rue Édouard VII

Rue Victor Emmanuel

Quai Quest

Rue Georges V

Bijouterie Balara

Alliance Française

La Boutique Cotona

Avenue du Colonel Gillon

Le Guest

Rue Maréchal Joffre

Rue Flacourt

Jardin Jean Ralaimongo

Rue Sylvain Roux

Consulat de Chine

Annexe CMMGM

Hôtel Maruti

Parad'Ice

Hôtel Fayyaaz

Nassib Hôtel

Bo S

Rue Flaco

Miguel Glace

Épicerie Tanjona

Mosquée Bohra

Mosquée Nouroul Islaam

Rue Jules Ferry

Lycée Al Noor

Rue André Chenier

Rue du Quai Orsini

Mini

Lolio Paris

Cercle Mess

Consulat de France à Majunga

Avenue Jules Aubourg

Tantsambo

Quai Orsini

Inn Majunga

Le Ravinala

Banky Foibe Mahajanga

Police Centrale

Ecole Nationale d'Enseignement Maritime

Water Front

Le Ravinala

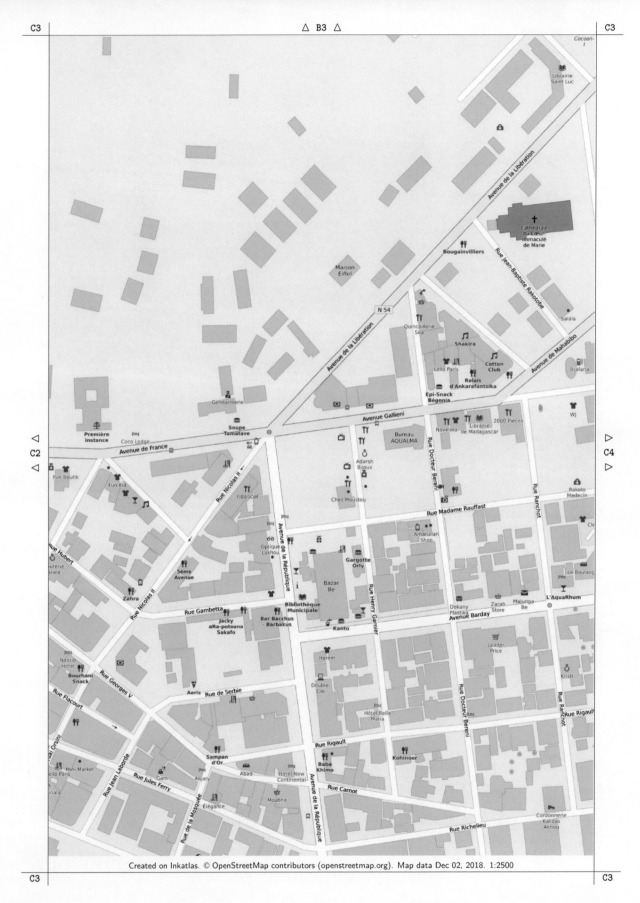

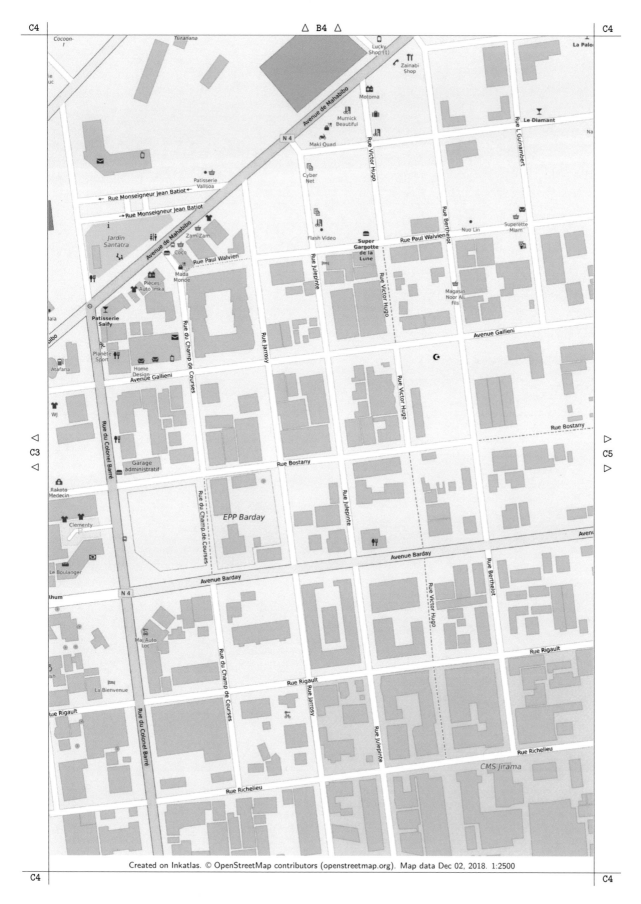

◁ C3 ◁

▷ C5 ▷

La Paloma

Le Majunga

Chez Ali
Baba

Pharmacie
Anais

Namana

Bain Douche;Epicerie
Camille

Rue Paul Walvien

Tantely

Mojumba
Hôtel

Pharmacie
du Centre

Avenue Galieni

Tranombarotra

ostany

Sapeurs-
Pompiers
Ville de
Mahajanga

Piste Rouge

Baobab

Avenue Barday

Bricodis

Avenue Barday

Avenue Barday

Boeny

Province de Mahajanga

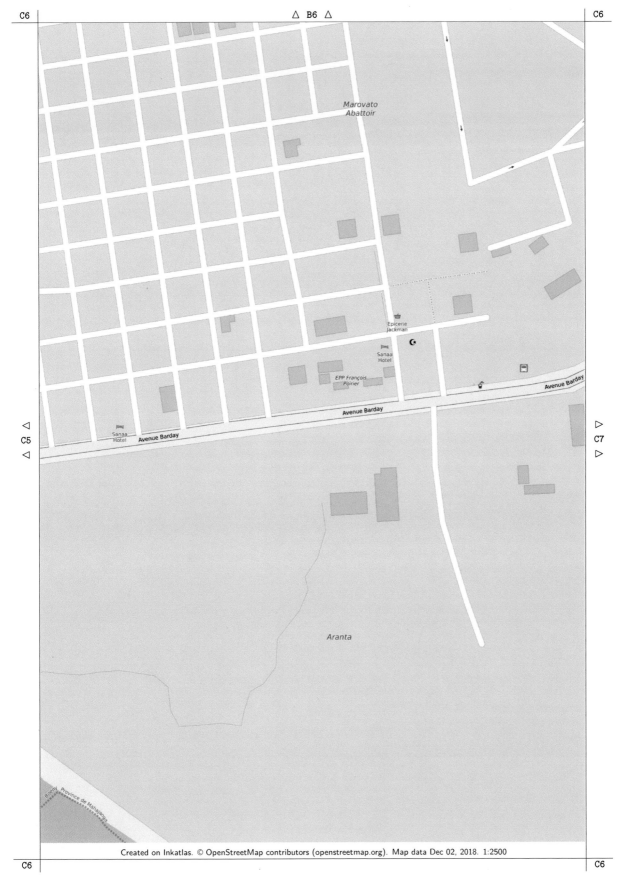

Marovato
Abattoir

Epicerie
Jackman

Sanaa
Hotel

EPP François
Poirier

Sanaa
Hotel

Avenue Barday

Avenue Barday

Avenue Barday

Aranta

Province de Mahajanga

Colis Express

Avenue Barday

Avenue Barday

ue Barday

Café de
la gare

# Travel Planner

WHERE?

_____

_____

_____

WHEN?

FROM: _____ / _____ / _____

TO: _____ / _____ / _____

DAYS: _____

TRANSPORTATION

☐ ✈ ☐ 🚌 ☐ 🚗 ☐ 🚤 ☐ 🚲 ☐ 🚶 ☐ _____

DETAILS:

_____

_____

_____

_____

_____

_____

_____

_____

_____

_____

_____

_____

_____

_____

Printed in Great Britain
by Amazon

87346052R00029

# Collins

# The Solar System

# sticker book

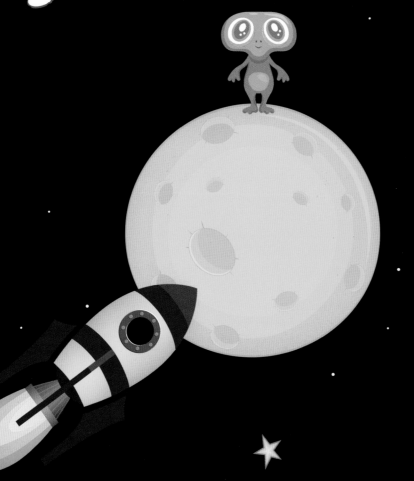

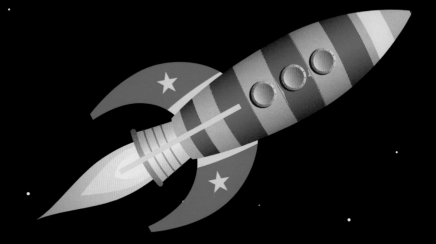

# Contents

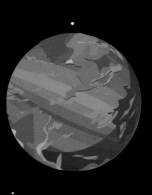

# The Solar System

"The Solar System is the Sun and the many objects that orbit it. These objects include eight planets, at least five dwarf planets and countless asteroids, meteoroids and comets. Orbiting some of the planets and dwarf planets are over 160 moons. The Sun keeps its surrounding objects in its orbit by its pull of gravity which has an influence for many millions of kilometres."

Sun

Astero Belt

Mercury

Earth

Venus

Mars

Meteoroid

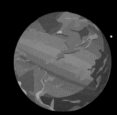

4

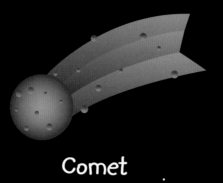

Comet

Jupiter

Uranus

Saturn

Neptune

# The Milky Way

"The Milky Way is the name of the spiral galaxy in which our Solar System is located. All the stars that we see in the night sky are part of the Milky Way galaxy. Aside from the relatively nearby stars, the galaxy appears as a hazy band of white light. The Solar System is located in the Milky Way halfway out from the centre."

The Milky Way

Our Solar System

# Inner Solar System

"There are four inner planets: Mercury, Venus, Earth and Mars. They are closest to the Sun and are known as the terrestrial planets because their surfaces are solid and rocky. The four planets are very different from each other and their surfaces are dotted with impact craters, valleys and some volcanoes. The Asteroid Belt is a region beyond the orbit of Mars where thousands of asteroids are found orbiting the Sun."

Uranus

Neptune

Asteroid
Belt

Jupiter

Saturn

Sun

EARTH

MERCURY

MARS

VENUS

## Mars

Named after the Roman god of war, it is often described as the "Red Planet".

## Earth

The only planet in the Solar System known to have life.

## Venus

Clouds of sulphuric acid prevent its surface being seen from Earth.

## Mercury

The smallest planet in the Inner Solar System.

# Mercury The Swift planet

"Mercury is the smallest planet. It is closest to the Sun and takes only eighty-eight Earth days to complete an orbit of the Sun. Mercury is scorching hot on its sunlit side, however it has no atmosphere to retain this heat so temperatures on its unlit side are extremely cold."

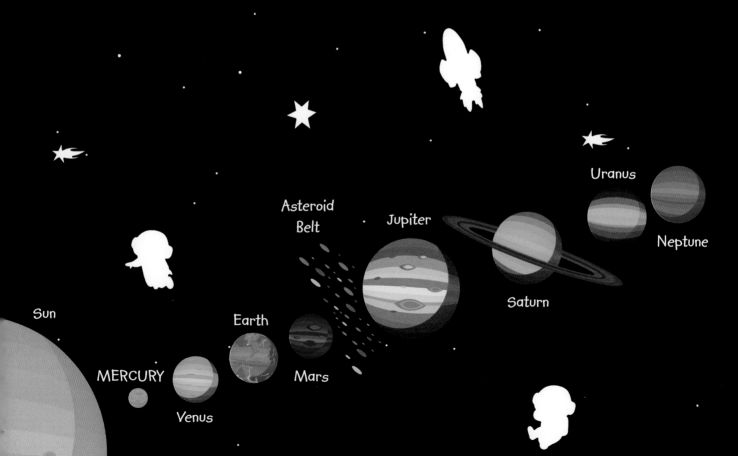

Uranus

Asteroid
Belt

Jupiter

Neptune

Saturn

Sun

Earth

MERCURY

Mars

Venus

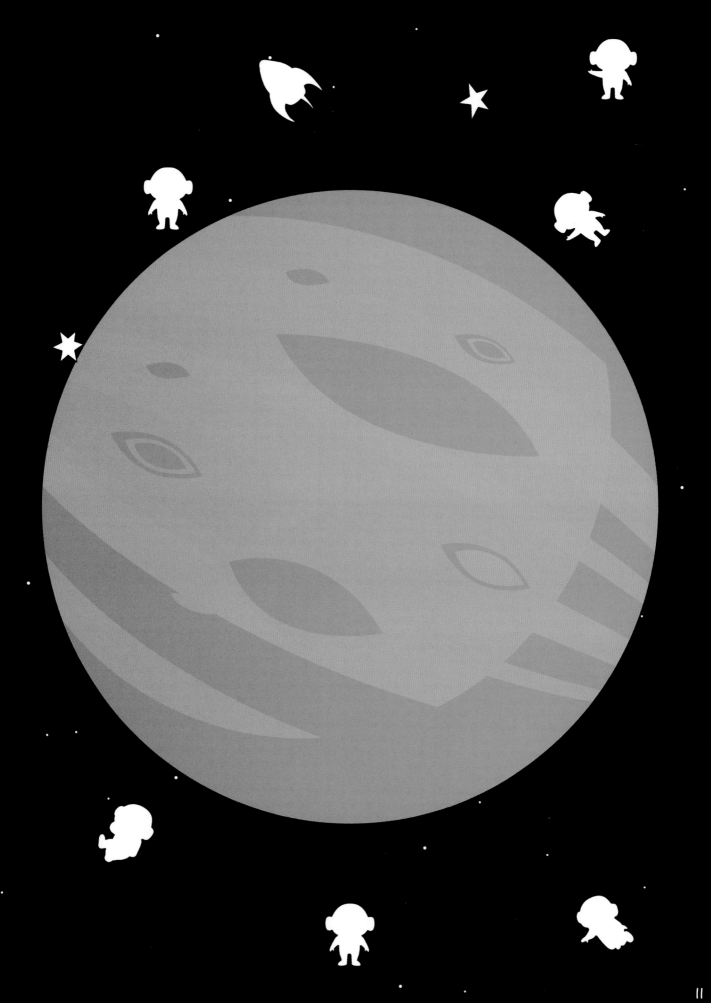

# Earth Our Home in Space

"Earth is the only planet in the Universe known to support life! It is a living planet, with plenty of water, trees, plants and breathable air, protected by its atmosphere. It is the third planet from the Sun and is the largest of the four rocky inner planets. Oceans, at least 4 kilometres deep, cover nearly 70 per cent of Earth's surface. It has one moon which is the only other place to be visited by people from Earth. It takes Earth 365 days and 6 hours (one year) to orbit the Sun."

Uranus

Asteroid Belt

Jupiter

Neptune

Saturn

Sun

EARTH

Mercury

Mars

Venus

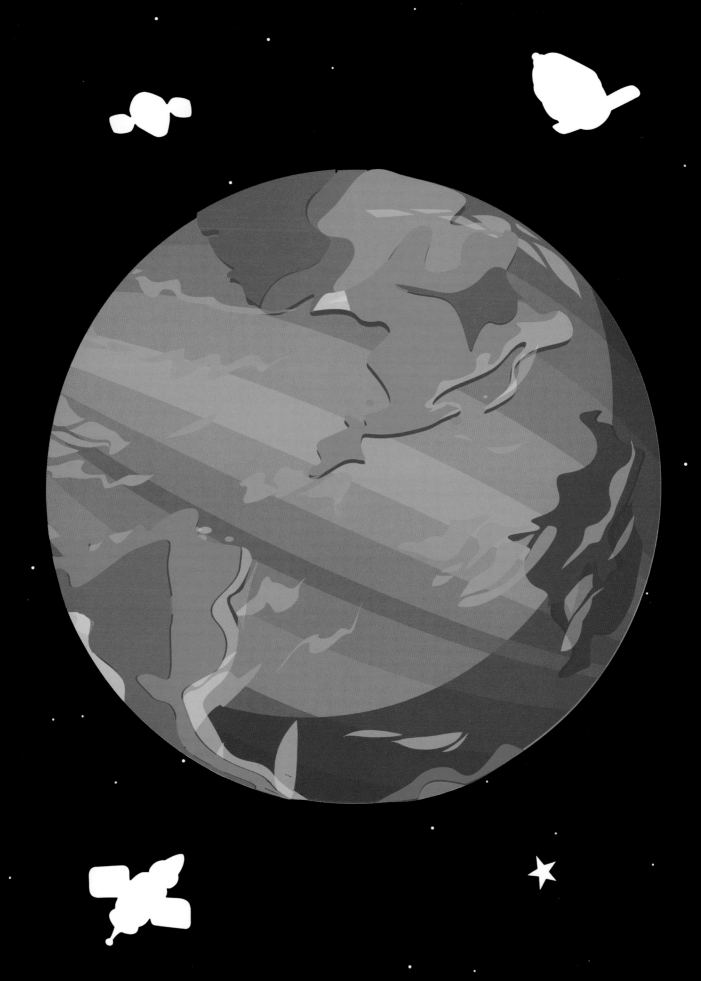

# Mars The Red Planet

"Mars is the fourth planet from the Sun and because of its blood red colour has been named after the Roman god of war. Its surface has been affected by volcanoes, crustal movements and dust storms. Mars has the tallest mountain in the Solar System, Olympus Mons, which rises 24 kilometres above the surrounding land."

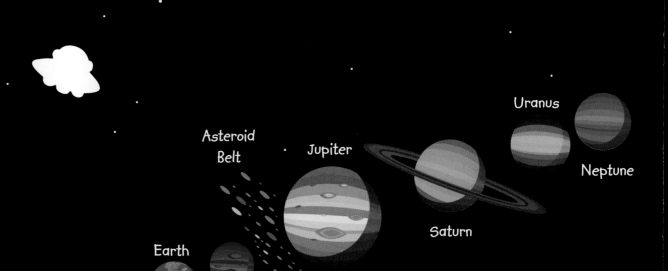

Sun

Mercury

Venus

Earth

MARS

Asteroid Belt

Jupiter

Saturn

Uranus

Neptune

# Outer Solar System

"The outer planets are: Jupiter, Saturn, Uranus and Neptune. They are sometimes known as the Gas Giants as they are huge in comparison to the inner planets and, made up mostly of gas, do not have solid surfaces. All four have rings around them, with Saturn's being the most famous. The four planets also have large numbers of moons orbiting them."

 URANUS

NEPTUNE

Asteroid Belt

JUPITER

SATURN

Sun

Earth

Mercury

Mars

Venus

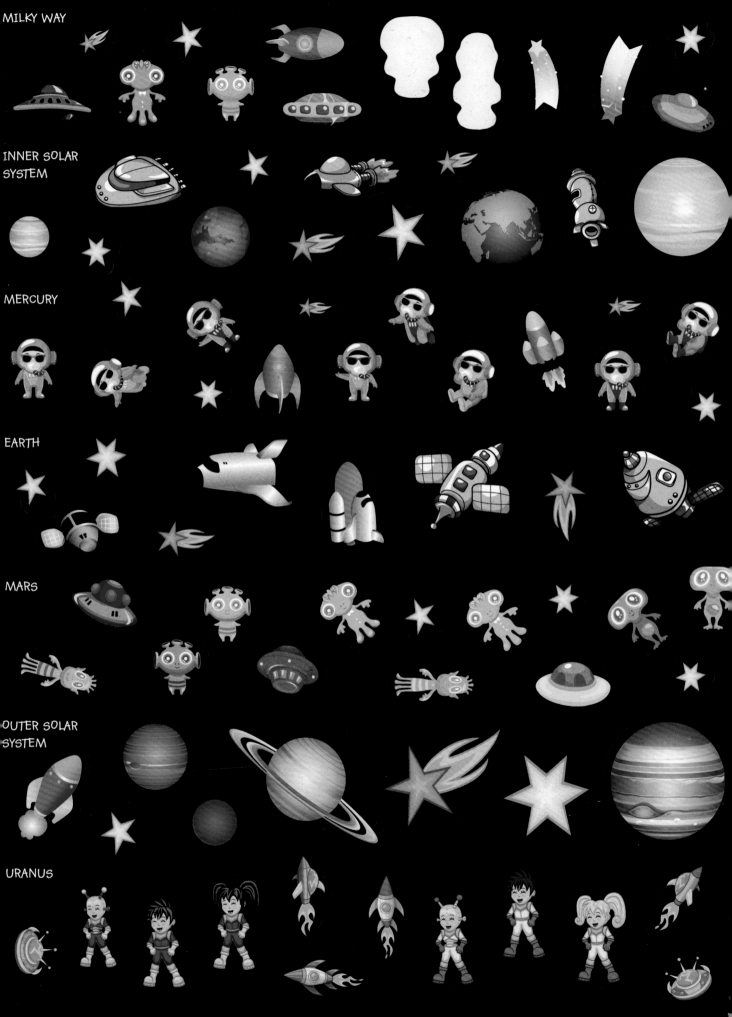

MILKY WAY

INNER SOLAR
SYSTEM

MERCURY

EARTH

MARS

OUTER SOLAR
SYSTEM

URANUS

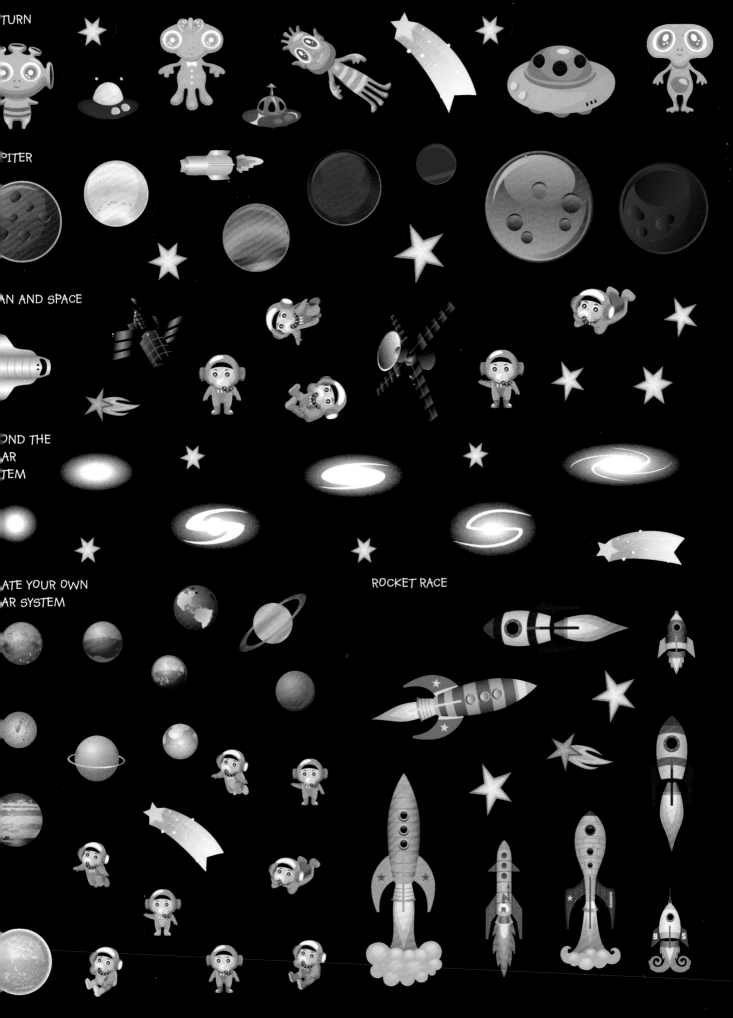

TURN

PITER

AN AND SPACE

OND THE
AR
TEM

ATE YOUR OWN
AR SYSTEM

ROCKET RACE

## Neptune
Named after the Roman god of the sea, it is the fourth largest planet

## Uranus
Uranus was the first planet discovered with a telescope

## Saturn
The rings of Saturn may be less than 10 metres thick in some places

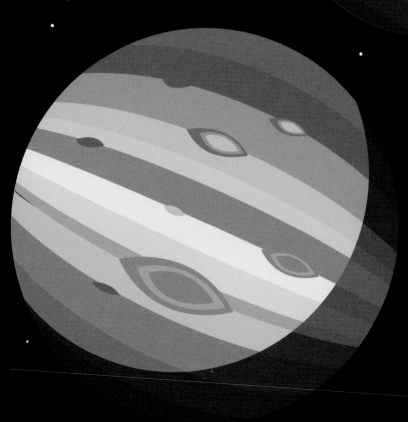

## Jupiter
The fifth planet from the Sun and the largest

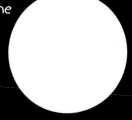

# Uranus The Blue Planet

"Uranus was first identified as a planet in 1781 by the British astronomer William Herschel. Uranus orbits the Sun on its side. This tipped rotational axis gives rise to extreme seasons on Uranus. It is thought that its unusual spin is due to a collision with another planet-sized object millions of years ago."

URANUS

Neptune

Asteroid
Belt

Jupiter

Saturn

Sun

Earth

Mercury

Mars

Venus

18

# Saturn The Ringed planet

"Saturn is the second largest planet in the Solar System. It is often called the ringed planet because it is surrounded by rings of dust and rocks. Like Jupiter, Saturn is a gas giant and is made up mainly of hydrogen. It is very light and if placed in a big pond of water it would float. Saturn spins very quickly. It takes only ten hours to rotate fully. A year on Saturn would take almost thirty Earth years. However, a day on Saturn is about ten and a half hours."

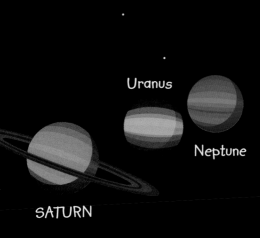

Uranus

Asteroid
Belt

Jupiter

Neptune

SATURN

Sun

Earth

Mercury

Mars

Venus

# Jupiter The Giant planet

"Jupiter is the largest planet in the Solar System. It is more than 300 times bigger than Earth. The planet is the fourth brightest object visible from Earth after the Sun, the Earth's moon and Venus. Its main feature is a Great Red Spot, which is a storm that has been going on for years. Jupiter has a ring system like all of the large gas planets, although these rings are not as famous or as visible as Saturn's. Orbiting Jupiter are at least sixty-three moons."

Uranus

Asteroid Belt

JUPITER

Neptune

Saturn

Sun

Earth

Mercury

Mars

Venus

# Man and Space

| Man lands on the Moon | | First space shuttle launch |
|---|---|---|
| 1957 - 1969 | 1970 - 1979 | 1980 - 1989 |

First space station

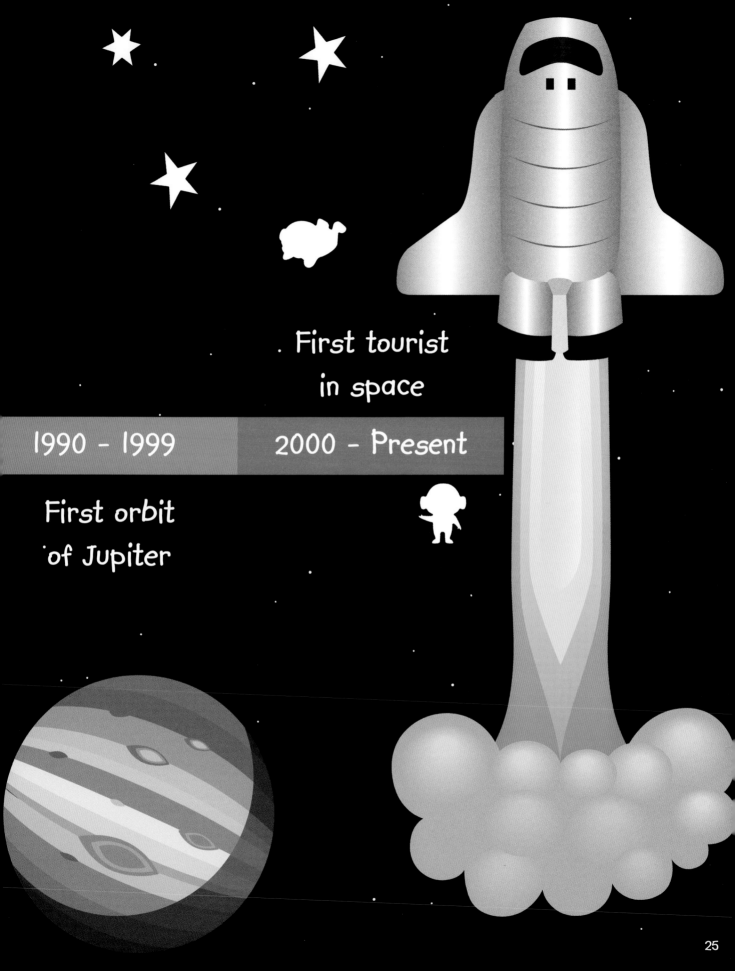

First tourist
in space

| 1990 - 1999 | 2000 - Present |

First orbit
of Jupiter

# Beyond the Solar System

"There is a lot more beyond the Solar System than eight planets, the Sun, moons and asteroids. Our galaxy is the Milky Way, however there are other galaxies, including the beautiful Andromeda Galaxy."

# ·TYPES OF GALAXIES

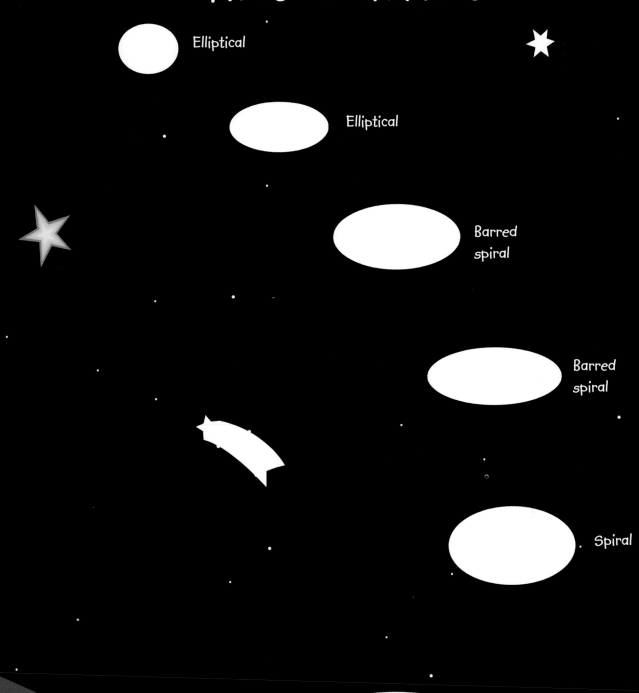

Elliptical

Elliptical

Barred spiral

Barred spiral

Spiral

Spiral

# Create your own Solar System

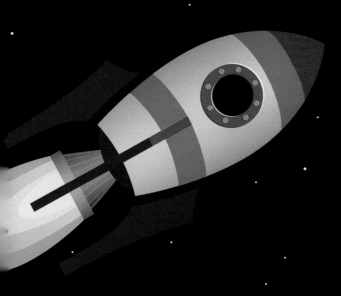

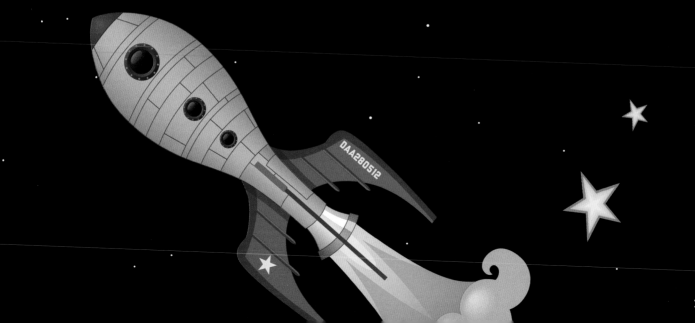

# Rocket Race

"Blast off! Which rocket will get to the moon first? Use stickers to create your very own rocket race!"

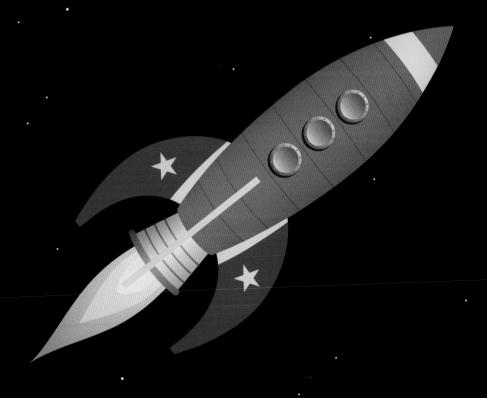

**COLLINS SOLAR SYSTEM**
Sticker Book

**Collins**
An imprint of HarperCollins Publishers
Westerhill Road
Bishopbriggs
Glasgow
G64 2QT

First Published 2013

Printed in China

ISBN 978-0-00-748142-2

Imp 003

Collins Bartholomew™,
the UK's leading independent geographical information
supplier, can provide a digital, custom, and premium
mapping service to a variety of markets.
For further information:
Tel: +44 (208) 307 4515
e-mail: collinsbartholomew@harpercollins.co.uk

or visit our website at: www.collinsbartholomew.com

**Image credits**

**Page 1** Genestro / Shutterstock.com, notkoo / Shutterstock.com, Bastetamon / Shutterstock.com

**Page 2 – 3** nobrand121876 / Shutterstock.com, 10 Year Bravo / Shutterstock.com,
Genestro / Shutterstock.com, notkoo / Shutterstock.com

**Page 4 –5** nobrand121876 / Shutterstock.com, 10 Year Bravo / Shutterstock.com

**Page 6 – 7** nobrand121876 / Shutterstock.com, 10 Year Bravo / Shutterstock.com, daulon / shutterstock.com

**Page 8 – 9** nobrand121876 / Shutterstock.com, 10 Year Bravo / Shutterstock.com

**Page 10 – 11** nobrand121876 / Shutterstock.com, 10 Year Bravo / Shutterstock.com

**Page 12 – 13** nobrand121876 / Shutterstock.com, 10 Year Bravo / Shutterstock.com

**Page 14 – 15** nobrand121876 / Shutterstock.com, 10 Year Bravo / Shutterstock.com, Klara Viskova / Shutterstock.com

**Page 16 – 17** nobrand121876 / Shutterstock.com, 10 Year Bravo / Shutterstock.com

**Page 18 – 19** nobrand121876 / Shutterstock.com, 10 Year Bravo / Shutterstock.com

**Page 20 – 21** nobrand121876 / Shutterstock.com, 10 Year Bravo / Shutterstock.com

**Page 22 – 23** nobrand121876 / Shutterstock.com, 10 Year Bravo / Shutterstock.com

**Page 24 – 25** nobrand121876 / Shutterstock.com, 10 Year Bravo / Shutterstock.com,
Anastasiia Kucherenko / Shutterstock.com, notkoo / Shutterstock.com, Genestro / Shutterstock.com

**Page 26 – 27** nobrand121876 / Shutterstock.com, 10 Year Bravo / Shutterstock.com,
Bastetamon / Shutterstock.com, notkoo / Shutterstock.com, Genestro / Shutterstock.com

**Page 28 – 29** Bastetamon / Shutterstock.com, Genestro / Shutterstock.com

**Page 30 – 31** nobrand121876 / Shutterstock.com, 10 Year Bravo / Shutterstock.com,
Genestro / Shutterstock.com, Koryaba / Shutterstock.com

**Page 32** Yulia M. / Shutterstock.com, barbaliss / Shutterstock.com,
Genestro / Shutterstock.com, notkoo / Shutterstock.com

**Stickers** stoyanh / Shutterstock.com, notkoo / Shutterstock.com, vectomart / Shutterstock.com,
Anastasiia Kucherenko / Shutterstock.com, Bastetamon / Shutterstock.com, Genestro / Shutterstock.com

**Cover** Alena Kozlova / Shutterstock.com, yusufdemirci / Shutterstock.com,
Anastasiia Kucherenko / Shutterstock.com, Bastetamon / Shutterstock.com,
Genestro / Shutterstock.com, notkoo / Shutterstock.com
Red spaceman unknown / Shutterstock.com

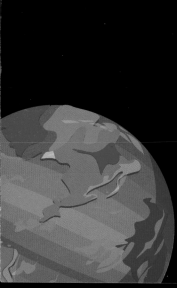